Wall painting at Hieranconpolis

The Art of Ancient Egypt

Shirley Glubok

designed by Gerard Nook

Atheneum   **1966**   *New York*

THE AUTHOR GRATEFULLY ACKNOWLEDGES THE KIND ASSISTANCE OF:

HENRY G. FISCHER, Assistant Curator, Department of Egyptian Art,
The Metropolitan Museum of Art.
ALAN RICHARD SCHULMAN, Assistant, Egyptian Section,
The University Museum, Philadelphia.
ROBERTA M. PAINE, Staff Lecturer, Junior Museum,
The Metropolitan Museum of Art.
MASTER BLAIR AXEL

Copyright © 1962 by Shirley Glubok
All rights reserved
Library of Congress catalog card number 62–10249
Published simultaneously in Canada by McClelland & Stewart Ltd.
Manufactured in the United States of America
Composition by Clarke & Way, New York
Printed by Connecticut Printers Inc., Hartford
Bound by H. Wolff, New York
First Printing June 1962
Second Printing March 1964
Third Printing October 1964
Fourth Printing March 1966

Title page illustration: The god Bes
Courtesy British Museum

Think back a year. It seems like a long time ago. It is hard to remember things that happened a year ago.

Try to think back five hundred years. America was just discovered about five hundred years ago.

Now try to think back five thousand years. At that time, in Egypt, there lived a remarkable people who created beautiful works of art. Many of these masterpieces still exist. We can see them in museums.

From the art in this book we can see how the Egyptians lived from sometime before 3100 B.C. until Roman times, about two thousand years ago.

Egypt is a hot, dry country in northern Africa. The great Nile River runs through the land. The soil is rich along the river. Plants grow along this narrow strip of land. But most of the country is desert.

The sun shines brightly and the sky is clear almost every day. However, far to the south of Egypt, where the Nile begins, it snows and rains. The melting snows and summer rains flow into the river.

Then as the Nile runs north, through Egypt, it rises and overflows its banks. When the floods are over in the fall, rich mud is left in the river valley. Without these floods there would be no crops and no food.

The yearly rise and fall of the Nile made it possible for people to live in Egypt. The lives of the people were centered about the river; and planting and harvesting were the subject of many wall paintings.

Wall painting at Thebes
Photograph by Egyptian Expedition
The Metropolitan Museum of Art

The ancient Egyptians enjoyed life. They believed that life could go on after death the same as it did before; and they wanted to keep on doing forever the things they enjoyed.

Kings and nobles had great stone tombs built for themselves. They believed that the spirit of the man lived on in his tomb. The walls of the tomb were painted with pictures of the things he liked to do.

The nobleman in this picture enjoyed hunting wild birds in the marshes of the Nile. While he was still alive, he had the picture painted in his tomb. He believed that after death magic powers would help him to enjoy hunting.

The artists who painted this picture had to follow certain rules, especially when they painted important people.

One rule was to paint a clear outline and fill in with color. Another was to paint the head and legs from the side, and the shoulders and eyes from the front. That is why you see parts of the front and side of the figure at the same time.

7

Some wall paintings show us that the artists did not always
follow their strict rules. When they painted everyday people,
they often painted lively, lifelike pictures.

The two dancers are carefree and seem to move to the music. Two of the musicians are shown looking out at us. It is also unusual to see the bottoms of feet in Egyptian painting.

The artist could be even more free when showing playful subjects. He could make them any way he liked.

It seemed amusing to this artist to paint a lion and an antelope sitting down and playing a board game and animals walking about like people.

This scene is part of a long scroll or roll. It is painted on papyrus. Papyrus is a plant that grows in the marshes of the Nile. Thin layers of the papyrus stalk were pressed together to make a material like paper. In fact, the word *paper* comes from *papyrus*.

This wall painting tells the story of a man who said some magic spells from the *Book of the Dead* and turned into a phoenix. He could do this whenever he wished. The phoenix was a sacred bird. As a phoenix, a dead man could go through the doors of his tomb and wander about outside.

The *Book of the Dead* was a book of magic spells to help the ancient Egyptian in his afterlife. It was drawn on a papyrus scroll.

13

One of the artist's important jobs was to decorate mummy cases. The Egyptians believed a person's body had to be preserved in order for him to enjoy life after death.

A mummy is a body wrapped in many layers of linen. It was put into a wooden mummy case. The case was in the form of a man. It had pictures of the gods and symbols painted on it to protect the mummy. A face, a wig, and jewelry were also painted on it.

Great care was taken to hide the mummy case. It was often placed at the bottom of a deep shaft. Yet tomb robbers usually found the cases and stole them for the jewelry and other precious treasures that were buried with them.

Outer coffin of Charioteer, Atef-Amon
The Metropolitan Museum of Art. Museum Excavations 1920–1921;
Rogers Fund and Contribution of Edward S. Harkness, 1921

Sometimes birds and animals were mummified, especially in late times. This
is the mummy case for a real bird. It is made of wood and over-laid with gold.
Its head and legs are silver.

Silver and gilt ibis
Courtesy Brooklyn Museum

15

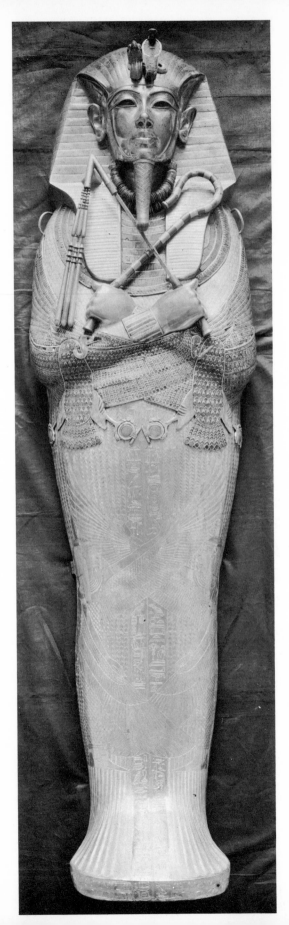

The now famous treasures of King Tut-ankh-Amun were safely hidden. They were put into a tomb that was cut into the side of a hill. The treasures were buried about 3,250 years ago.

The body of the young king was put into this mummy case. It was then covered by two other mummy cases. This case is pure gold and weighs over nine hundred pounds. Beautiful stones are laid into the gold to make it sparkle. The eyebrows and eyelids are inlaid with sparkling blue glass. The false beard is a symbol of his kingly rank. The cobra and the vulture on his headdress are also kingly symbols.

The magnificent gold mask at the right lay over the head of the mummy. It was inside the three mummy cases. It is fitting that King Tut-ankh-Amun's face looks young, because he died when he was about eighteen years old.

17

Important people also had statues made of themselves. The statue would take the place of the mummy if it should be destroyed.

Just as there were rules for painting, there were rules for making statues. Only a few dignified poses were used. Statues might stand or sit. But there could be no twist to the body.

Queen Hat-shepsut sits on her throne with her feet firmly on the ground. Her hands rest on her knees. She looks straight ahead. These were the kind of rules that were made for seated statues.

The Metropolitan Museum of Art. Rogers Fund and Contribution of Edward S. Harkness, 1926

King Mycerinus follows the rules for standing statues. He walks barefoot with his left foot forward. He wears a crown and a kilt. He looks calm and powerful.

Hathor, the cow-goddess, with horns, stands on one side of him. The goddess on the other side represents one of the King's provinces. The jackal above her is the symbol of the province. They have their arms around the King, to show their affection.

One of the great pyramids was built for Mycerinus.

Cairo Museum
Photograph by Carol Guyer

An Egyptian king liked to show his power. So he would have statues made of his own head on the body of a crouching lion. This is called a *sphinx*. It shows that the king is as strong as a lion.

This pink granite sphinx guarded the entrance to Queen Hat-shepsut's temple.

Very few women ruled Egypt. A woman had no right to rule. A queen gave her son the right to rule; but she herself was only a "king's wife." Queen Hat-shepsut ruled by calling herself *king*.

Her stepson was angry with her because he thought he should be king. When she died, he ordered all of her statues broken. They were not pieced together again until modern times.

The Metropolitan Museum of Art
Photograph by Alfred H. Tamarin
Museum Excavations 1926–1928

Egyptians believed in many gods. Bes, the household god, was one of their favorites. Many statues were made of him.

He is savage-looking, with a big head and eyes. But he was thought to be a kind, friendly god who watched over women and children.

Bes is a creature, part man and part lion. He keeps his mouth open, and his tongue hangs out. Here, he rests one paw on an emblem that means he is protecting the home.

Cairo Museum
Photograph by Harry Burton,
The Metropolitan Museum of Art

The Egyptians thought that their gods could take the form of a bird or an animal. Horus, a sky god, could take the form of a hawk.

Here he is represented as the god of kingship. He wears the royal crown. In this case he is connected with King Nectanebo, who is shown in front of him.

Horus had four sons who were friendly spirits. They watched over the four points of the compass: north, east, south, and west.

These little statues of the four sons are only four inches tall. Their bodies are shaped like mummies. Their heads are those of a jackal, a human, a hawk, and an ape.

At the left is part of a seated statue of King Chephren. The statue's face is wonderfully carved from a very hard stone. He looks grand and powerful. Horus is now connected with King Chephren. Horus protects the king with his spreading wings.

Amun was one of the most important gods of Egypt. This beautiful little statue at the right follows the rules for standing statues. He holds a curved sword against his chest as a symbol of victory.

The statue of Amun is smaller than this picture. It is only seven and a half inches high. It is made of gold. Few gold statues remain because most of them were melted down for the valuable metal.

This bust of Queen Nefretite was found in an ancient Egyptian sculptor's studio. It was used as a model to make other statues. It is so beautiful that many copies of it are still being made.

The Queen wears her crown. The eye is inlaid with rock crystal. This bust is painted in bright colors.

The goddess Neith was the guardian of warriors and hunters. This statue is carved of wood and is painted gold. It protected a shrine in Tut-ankh-Amun's tomb. There were four goddesses protecting the shrine, one at each corner. We know this one is Neith by the symbol on her head.

Plaster cast of a painted limestone original
The Metropolitan Museum of Art
Rogers Fund, 1925 (original now in Berlin)

Cairo Museum
Photograph by Harry Burton,
The Metropolitan Museum of Art

In the early days, cats were wild, like lions. Later, cats were tamed and became family pets.

Bastet, goddess of love and joy, took the form of a female cat when she walked on earth. She was a merry goddess who practiced magic. People wore little cat charms to bring them good luck. This bronze cat wears a woman's gold earrings because she is a goddess.

This strange head is on a bed that was found in Tut-ankh-Amun's tomb. It looks fierce, but it really represents a kind and friendly creature.

The head is carved out of wood and is painted gold. It wears a royal headdress.

Not all animal statues represented gods. Hunting hippopotamuses was a great sport in early Egyptian times. This jolly hippopotamus was put into a tomb, perhaps to bring the hunter good hunting in his afterlife. This statue is made of faience, a material something like pottery. It is covered with a glaze. Lotus flowers on the body show that the hippopotamus is standing in a marsh.

Fish are common in Egyptian art because the Nile River played a very important part in Egyptian life. This little fish is a small bottle. Its mouth is the opening of the bottle. It is made of colored glass.

The Metropolitan Museum of Art
Rogers Fund, 1915

Besides the wall paintings, the ancient Egyptians filled the tombs with real food, jewelry, and furniture. Sometimes they put in little models of people at work, to serve them in their afterlife.

We think this model is a groom taking care of his master's horse. It was unusual for an Egyptian to ride a horse. Horses usually were used to pull chariots.

This model is a servant woman carrying a basket of food and a duck for her master. He was a wealthy nobleman named Meket-Re.

Luckily Meket-Re hid his models in a secret room. Most of his tomb was robbed. But the secret room was not discovered until March 17, 1920.

The Metropolitan Museum of Art
Excavated by Egyptian Expedition of the
Metropolitan Museum of Art, 1919–1920;
Rogers Fund and Contribution of Edward S. Harkness

Like most Egyptians, Meket-Re spent a great deal of time on the Nile. This is his fishing and fowling boat. He is sitting with his son. Servants bring them fowl. The men fish with harpoons.

Meket-Re's sailing boat is fully rigged. The men are at work with the sail and the tiller. The captain holds a staff. His head is shaved. But the rest of the crew have thick hair on their heads to protect them from the hot sun.

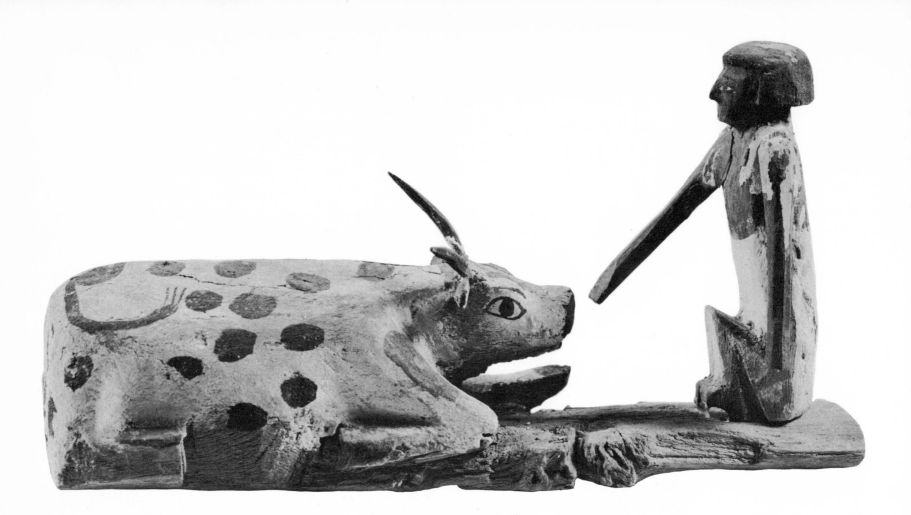

Great care was taken to make these little wooden models lifelike. They tell us a great deal about how people lived in Egypt four thousand years ago.

This is a model of a man feeding an ox. It is from the tomb of another noble.

This is another group of models from the tomb of Meket-Re. Servants are bringing him supplies. The first man carries a vase on his shoulder and an incense burner in his hand. The second man brings sheets. The last two are women, carrying food.

The Egyptians used their art to decorate everyday objects. This vase is from pre-historic times. It is made of Nile clay. The vase is decorated with goats and flamin-goes. The triangles stand for mountains. The wavy lines may stand for water.

This lovely bowl is also made of clay. It is covered with a glaze. It is decorated with lotus flowers and a double emblem of Hathor, the cow-goddess. The decoration fits the shape of the bowl nicely.

The ancient Egyptians liked to spend many hours making themselves attractive. They rubbed their skins with oils and perfumes. Both men and women painted their eyelashes and eyebrows. The oils and eye make-up helped protect them from the hot sun. They had beautiful containers for their make-up.

The "blue marble" monkey is a vase for eye-paint. His head is the lid. He holds a small jar.

The swimming girl is a make-up spoon. She stretches her arms to hold on to a gazelle that seems to pull her along in the water. The top of the gazelle comes off. The inside is hollow to hold make-up.

Highly polished metal was used for mirrors. This mirror has a gold handle in the shape of a papyrus stalk. The face is that of Hathor, the cow-goddess.

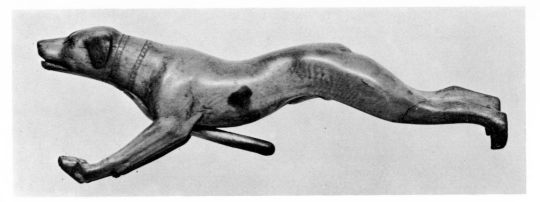

Ancient Egyptian children liked pets and toys, just as children do today.

The ivory dog above is a mechanical toy. A rod is attached to his lower jaw. When a child pressed the rod, the dog's mouth opened.

Board games were very popular. The one below is senet. It is the oldest type of board game we know.

The Metropolitan Museum of Art
Hound; Rogers Fund, 1940
"Senet"; Gift of Egyptian Exploration Fund, 1901

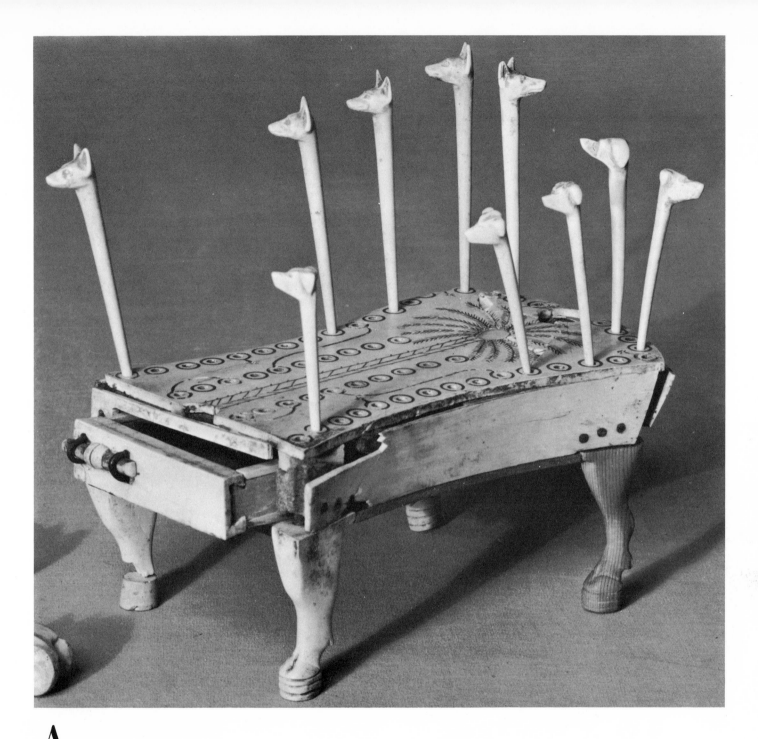

Another board game called "hounds and jackals" was played like parcheesi.

The playing pieces are five hounds, with ears down, and five jackals, with ears up.

They were moved from hole to hole. Knucklebones were used for dice.

"Hounds and Jackals"; Carnarvon Collection,
Gift of Edward S. Harkness, 1926

The stone tablet at the left shows Egyptian picture writing. It looks like many little drawings. They are called *hieroglyphs*. Each picture stands for a sound, a group of sounds, or sometimes an entire word. There were hundreds of different picture symbols in Egyptian hieroglyphic writing.

The Metropolitan Museum of Art
Hieroglyphs; Funds from the Huntley Bequest, 1959

Courtesy University Museum, Philadelphia

The writing on the papyrus scroll above is from a *Book of the Dead*. When the Egyptians wrote on papyrus they usually drew the pictures quickly. This quicker kind of writing is called *hieratic*. Hieroglyphs can be compared to our printing. Hieratic can be compared to our script.

Only a few people knew how to read and write in ancient Egypt. Educated people were called *scribes*. The scribe at the left sits with an open papyrus scroll on his knees.

Since the ancient Egyptians believed that life could go on forever, even after death, they wanted their writings and their art treasures to last for all time. The sand and the dry desert air of Egypt have preserved some of them for more than five thousand years. The huge pyramids in Egypt can last for thousands of years to come.

Perhaps these ancient people have had their wish, after all.